Appreciations

"In precise language and varied f
of poetry, *Stage Whispers*, welcomes readers into thoughtful narrative observations that are personal and political, serious and lighthearted. Like the multitude of grasses on the Kansas prairie, these handsomely crafted poems are grounded in nature's deep richness and beauty yet contemplate Christianity, science, and humanity, dragonflies, stars, morels, red-tailed hawks, the snows of Badakhshan, sandhill cranes, and great blue herons, all balanced against God riding by on his bicycle. Dense with images, intimate and honest, the book urges in brilliant whispers for readers to embrace life, to 'Inhale deeply. / Breathe.'"

—Kathryn Kysar, author of *Dark Lake* and *Pretend the World*

"Roy Beckemeyer's new book of poems, *Stage Whispers*, speaks from on, off, below, and above the stage of life . . . showing us how to hear what we have to say to the world, and what the world is saying to us. From the first poem, beginning with the lines, 'When the wind sends your words back/ into your throat as you speak them,' Beckemeyer once again shows us the essential nature of listening closely to the music and quiet of everyday rhythms, yearnings, connections, losses, and motions. He writes with originality and precision about the natural world, growing up in the Midwest, old friends and old places that shaped lives, and even the workings of our minds, telling us in 'Electrifying Thoughts' that if we could see our own neurons in action, 'We'd be meteor showers. We'd/ be each other's very own auroras.' But the most powerful cord that threads through this book is love: love for being alive to witness the tilting of seasons and weather, both external and internal, as well as love for the moments and humans that illuminate our days. As he writes in 'Above the Rocky Run,' 'The whole world could rush by in flood stage / and whirlpools and every bit of it / would be immaterial with you in sight, / this close to hand.' Speaking of which, keep this book close at hand to better see what and who is coming onto the stage of your life."

—Caryn Mirriam-Goldberg, 2009-13 Kansas Poet Laureate, and author of *Everyday Magic: Fieldnotes on the Mundane and Miraculous*

"In this new volume of work by a treasured Kansas poet, Roy Becke-meyer takes the reader to historic rural settings, the nature of farm and prairie. These poems are lean yet muscled with the intense track of a quail hunt, the rise and rustle of prey, the sudden fall to ground . . . I applaud *Stage Whispers* as an artistic voice that calls us all to savor this collection from a skilled craftsman of modern verse."

—Gary Lechliter, author of *Off the Beaten Path*

"Roy Beckemeyer's *Stage Whispers* invites us to see the lively currents that underpin our world. His wide-ranging eye examines everything from the microscopic to the cosmic and reports back to us a universe filled with brightness and worthy of our close attention"

—Skyler Lovelace, poet and artist, Professor of Digital Media and owner of *Pixel Time*

"Like his 2015 Kansas Notable Book *Music I Once Could Dance To*, Roy Beckemeyer's third book of poetry, *Stage Whispers*, sings. . . . *Stage Whispers*' melody follows nature's beauty, from forests to in-sects, weather to birds— 'You know you have perfect pitch / when you can transcribe / the brown thrasher's morning song.' It contains the murmur of bees who turn the golden light of summer into honey and trees that 'toss leaves into the sky.' 'When Is It Summer in Kansas?' Beckemeyer asks, '. . . when storm clouds say with lightning what they refuse to speak with rain' These are poems that offer a new pitch on viewpoints that limit, 'the storm fronts that we invent and then must learn to weather' . . . To hear how a poet like Roy Beckemeyer heals unexpected wounds with unexpected beauty, listen to *Stage Whis-pers*."

—Laura Madeline Wiseman, author of *Through a Certain Forest*

Stage Whispers

POETRY

Roy J. Beckemeyer

Stage Whispers
Copyright © 2018 Roy J. Beckemeyer

Meadowlark (an imprint of Chasing Tigers Press)
P.O. Box 333
Emporia, Kansas 66801
meadowlark-books.com

Roy J. Beckemeyer
royjbeckemeyer.com
royjbeckemeyer@gmail.com

Digital art for the cover and chapter headings
whispering persona masks by Roy J. Beckemeyer.

ISBN: 978-1-7322410-3-9

Library of Congress Control Number: 2018952846

Stage
Whispers

POETRY

Roy J. Beckemeyer

A MEADOWLARK BOOK

Also by Roy J. Beckemeyer:

Music I Once Could Dance To
Amanuensis Angel

For Melanie,
Fellow Wayward Poet –

*Dedicated to my fellow Wayward Poets, current
and past; we are each other's audience, cast
members, and critics.*

*Here's to our mutual
love of words and poems.
Thanks!*

"All the world's a stage and most of us are desperately unrehearsed."

~ Seán O'Casey

Table of Contents

"imaginary circumstances" · 41

"Every scene you will ever act begins in the middle, and it is up to you, the actor, to provide **what comes before**."

~ Michael Shurtleff

When Is It Summer in Kansas?

When the wind sends your words back
into your throat as you speak them.

When the sun banks its heat up
under your hat brim, and the cool
of morning is lost in months past.

When robins thirst thirteen ways
for water, and the first cicada
rasps at the heat before noon.

When leaves curl and click rather
than brush against one another
in the breeze, and turtles scratch
at parched earth for moisture.

When heat wavers above roads
in spasms, and farmers disk
spindly wheat back into dusty ground.

When foxes dig their dens
a little deeper, and earthworms
are nowhere to be found.

When storm clouds say with lightning
what they refuse to speak with rain.

Lyric

I would sing of hard men shaped
by shoveling coal, men with
black smudges on their faces
and hands, of smoke billowing
from smelter stacks, whistles
sounding across town at shift change,
of union dues and lunch pails,
of cooling ponds empty of fish,
of night shifts and night trains,
rolling steel wheels under loads
of anthracite, loads of zinc.

I would sing of general stores
with ledger books and every-other-Friday
paychecks, pails of beer, poker games,
trot lines and beat up cars,
of shining scuffed shoes on Saturday,
attending church on Sunday,
of sick kids and healthy kids,
of school nights, of summer days
spent in garden rows pulling weeds.

I would sing of how I traipsed
in a man's path, my scrawny arms
swinging, shoes untied, trying
to ape his confident step,
hearing everyone who passed
joke and smile and call out
greetings to him.

I would sing of my father.

Illinois Days

1

Along those gravel roads,
ditches puddled with May rain,
dewberry canes ran rampant.
Chorus frogs kvelled plainchant
to morning. The sun split clouds
like layers of mica, scattered its gold
lavishly at us—the day's beggars—
not knowing we would have settled
for less—accustomed as we were
to the pinchpenny ways of the world.

2

I stalked your lanky-legged
adolescence through corn rows,
innocently set clouds of pollen free
to float, find, settle onto, and gild
the intimate tassels of your hair.

3

In our orchard bees droned in squadrons
through long, amber-shadowed
avenues of evening; apple trees
cloud-banked into blossom
on every side. Pollen and nectar
accumulated in reservoirs of wax;
air throbbed and surged with alchemy:
bees transforming all that gold
into honey.

Spring, Bittersweet as Separation

O. Henry surprises await
slipstream girls, exuberant boys;

pear blossom confetti shreds
like words left dangling in autumn;

pencil-sharp tulip leaves pierce
through winter's remnants;

wind gusts like sneezes. Draw it all
with words and phrases. Chalk

it onto sidewalks, hop-scotch
a barrage of April notes.

Oh, this keyboard path, oh
these chromatic dancing days.

First Holy Communion

Children of God dressed in white
so bright the sun makes each face
appear to hover in the dazzling air:
Angelic, perplexed, worried,
content—already floating as if
to set off heavenward—
a day of peace.

But the truce would be broken
on the playground tomorrow
by the one kid unwilling
to change, unable to float
skyward, still anchored
by the need to bully.

His slight smile is already angling
toward trademark smirk,
here on the very day
when God came
and sat on his tongue,
and he swallowed,
waited for the lightning that never
came, knew then that he
could continue to be himself,
as he had always been,
as he was now,
would be tomorrow,
and forevermore.

Family

*A Golden Shovel Poem after
Gwendolyn Brooks' "We Real Cool"*

There was no such thing as spare change. We
didn't ask for pennies for candy. We really
did know the score. If we wanted heat on cool
mornings we needed to bank the fire at night. We
ate what was on our plates; there were no left-
overs. We walked through snow and rain to school.
Arrived on time, mostly, although some days we
dawdled—especially me. I would find a way to lurk
out of site, in an alley, and then get to school late.
Sometimes I look back and wonder how it is we
poor kids made it through. We were strike-
out kings, I suppose. We seemed set to go straight
from school to work for *ASARCO*. But dad fixed that. We
went together to the smelter. His friends would sing
out "Hey, Pal!" I thought he had it all. "It would be a sin,"
he said, "for you to work here. Look at us. We
break our backs shoveling coal. Paycheck too damn thin
to pay our bills. Might as well rub a lamp, expect a *Jinn*
to grant our wishes. You need school. Your mom and I, we
want more for you." He liked country music, so I chose jazz.
I didn't know that he would be gone, that year, by June.
The leukemia took him quickly. It seems now that we
barely had a father. He was too damned young to die.
You think you have a world of time, but it ends so soon.

Great Blue Heron,

dead snag along the edge of the creek,
unfolds like a parasol opening,
squawks effort, pulls
gangly
 legs
  that
   trail
    like
     reeds
        behind her,
        white lime of feces
        streak onto water like
        an afterthought
        wide wings mask
        the road of sky
        between the trees,
        a deep whoosh
        so thick with flapping
        you suck at your breath,
        cramp your diaphragm
        to catch and swallow
        that air before it
        curls away into
        the eddies of
        her leaving.

Stand by Me

Walking rails,
arms extended—
four of us
in tandem—
leaning as much
in response to the kid
ahead as to our own
swaying need
for equilibrium.
We rock with each
gust like hovering
hawks, count ties
as our measure
of progress.

The sun-burnished metal
works its heat
through the soles
of our sneakers,
the rail extends off
into the haze of horizon,
approaches but never
touches its parallel
companion,
points the way
to the future, the one
that at our age has no
end, that seems laid out
and straight-forward,
solid as lengths of steel
spiked to slabs
of tarred wood.

En Passant

Recalling Irwin Shaw's short story,
"The Girls in Their Summer Dresses"

At the periphery
                of his eye
        a liquid   sway   of hem,
                a carousel-whirl
                of skirt   edge,
        the dance   of weave
                    to gravity
                    and air, earth-
            pull and viscous
                    vorticity,
        membrane   stresses, fabric
            modalities.   Pleats   open,
        close,
            shed   concertina notes
                    that   flutter
                        in her wake.

            Her legs   brush   the
                cymbal-cloth of her
                        flaring   skirt.
        The   gentle   concavity
                    of softness   behind
                her knee
                    flirts   with each
                        sundress   stride.
        She rounds the corner.   A swish,
                            a lingering tone, ·
                    a rustling,
            a decrescendo.

Anderson Creek Creed

*After reading Bronwen Butter Newcott's
"Creed in the Santa Ana Winds"*

You did not believe that red cedars could
transform themselves explosively into flame:
an earthly form of transubstantiation

("Forgive me, Father," you say, as you think
that thought); that you would cut fences, praying
your cattle might outrun the torrent of fire;

that your truck's headlights would flare like
molten lava; that flames would *jeté*
over roads, over dozer-scraped pasture;

that fickle winds would conspire to find fresh fuel
for fire; that you would find haven at last in new
winter wheat, slight and green and beneath the flame's

fierce notice, fenced by walls of black smoke, by
skeletal trees clutching at the sky for relief,
by stars gone dizzy with hot air and soot;

that God would wait until your faith began
to smolder, to crisp around its edges,
before finally bestowing the benison of rain.

The Colors of Song

"...I hear the birds singing in my
backyard
I guess the color of their feathers..."
—Xánath Caraza, from
her poem "It Is Winter"

the red-tailed hawk
brandishes his bright
keeeeerrrr, a light saber
gleaming, silvered,
fluorescent

when starling song
gurgles like water
over stones, the sun
strokes their feathers
with mist-borne iridescence

chickadee *zeee's*
make jagged Zorro
strokes of black lightning,
their masks hide
bright eyes

the high notes
of the creeper approach
the stratosphere,
blue so pale you might
mistake it for white

Dew Point

Porch lights squint star patterns
into morning mist,

windows curtained with condensate
blink on with shy grace.

Trees take on the magic
of floatation.

Down the street joggers weave
spirit manifestations—

their pony tails flicker
in the foggy dawn.

Baseball

Spherical aims
almost achieved,
flexing its ball
of twine fullness,

cork its resilient,
hidden inmost
heart, its Holstein-
hide bleached

to a stunning white,
it sports the natty
red numerology
of its doubled stitches,

nine-dozen exact,
lives in two leagues
of its own, longs
to be knuckled,

two-seamed, four-
seamed, sliding,
slicing, slurving
toward home.

Grain Elevator Gray

*A Golden Shovel poem
inspired by Liz Berry's
"Birmingham Roller"*

The elevator towers at the edge of town;
grain-dust hovers when hard-red winter wheat is cut.

The combines chew lanes; the trucks have no wings,
yet fly over gravel roads. This year's crop was chest-

deep on the young men whose faces are now dust
covered. They rent rooms without clothes-cabinets,

small town antiquated tourist cabins: men
who will not turn home till winter. Feathers

of the pigeons are dirt-colored. Dust-gray eggs
fill their nests now; the birds almost tumble

as they swoop to peck up spilled kernels. Terraces
step foreign fields but here flatness reigns and you

watch the birds soar over heat-baked ground through
the sun's bright notice. They absorb June so that January

will not cut so deep. They will move south later, yo-yo
back with spring, desperate gray against white clouds.

Above the Rocky Run

I aim my kayak catty-corner to
the current, ferry across toward you.

You cling to hickory roots that hang
over the bank, become an anchor of sorts,
your slender arm roped with tensed muscle.

Sunlight skips across the riffles.
Your boat is lit along its length
by dancing sparks, its green
prow, cutting the stream, curls
rushing water away, twirls it into
diverging wet spirals.

You balance at the brink of instability,
a pull or push away from turning bank-
ward or whirling downstream, a barely
acute angle from awkward and tilting
imbalance, a mere tenuous misjudgment
away from losing the streamlined perfection
of this moment.

You live your whole life like this,
exquisitely balanced between grounding
and going orbital, grinding to a halt or
achieving escape velocity, and I aim my path,
my trajectory, just as always, toward the center
of your gravity, the epitome of your being.

The whole world could rush by in flood stage
and whirlpools and every bit of it
would be immaterial with you in sight,
this close to hand.

—for Pat and all the rivers we shared

Staying Warm

We shove slender
lengths of cast-off,
bark-skinned log-edges
onto the truck bed,
the feral screech of green
wood against rusted metal
dissonant as the shriek
of sawmill blade tearing
lumber shapes and sawdust
from the hearted trunks
of flood-plain walnut,
oak, pecan.

At home, our own
blade voices its hunger
as we cross-cut slabs
for firewood. Stacks
scaffold shed walls higher
with each succeeding trip.
Spiders, mice, and beetles
find, between these fragrant
layers, lacunae for lasting
out the winter.

Three armloads stoke
the fire for the dark
descent of night,
fill the stove's belly
with coals that glow
through its isinglass
navel, that slowly turn
gray as they give back
what it is they remember
of heaven's sun.

jack 1941-1959

flying off the levee road at 85 or so
his '48 plymouth scraped bark off a sycamore
    nosed over   and flipped
  top down into muck   wheels   spinning
    he had no chance the stupid fuck   the
state trooper said   the next day we all drove together
to see   back behind the body shop
  right-side-up   roof shoved down into
the seats   no blood just dirt
  oh shit was all anyone could say
he was still there in the yearbook   but
   wouldn't be tossing his cap   into the air
      at graduation

         remember
  them slick hunting knives he made
  in his dad's shop?   asked frankie   and i
   nodded   felt my thumb scraping
the blade   hefting the damned lovely
balance of the thing before i handed
over a month's gas money   to buy it
   remembered   jack's open-mouth grin
   as i whistled at the craft   he put into it

      hell   none of us
  could believe it till the funeral home
with   doreen crying   and his dad red-eyed
  and jack's hair combed back   in that
duck tail he liked   and dammit his eyes
were closed almost like the cool way   he would squint
   because of smoke from the pall mall
   that was always hanging at the corner
of his mouth   but so tight now there   was no way
he would see us again   and his mouth   was closed too
  and there was no way   he was ever going to tell
      any of us
        why

"... acting ... allows you to live **other people's lives** without having to pay the price."

~ Robert De Niro

Ruby (1954)

You always wear men's pants, un-tucked work shirt.
I once asked dad why. He just shuffled his feet, said
"More comfortable, I guess."

A *Camel* dangles from your lower lip.
You chalk your cue, tell old man Solis again
what a lousy eight-ball player he is, smirk, hunker over,
line up your shot, grind your cigarette into the floor,
stretch over the table.

Your hair falls in your eyes, a comb-over, barber shop style,
same sandy-brown color as your scuffed men's shoes.
You tilt up onto your toes, the shirt falls away. I see a hint
of slender waist.

My illusion of you as shapeless falters a bit,
but then you straighten up, spit reality
into your empty beer bottle, shift the chaw
around in your cheek.

Here, in the tavernous darkness
of this no-stoplight small town, you
are pig's-feet-in-brine-on-the-bar real,
swaggering, boisterous, cussing real,
never-leaving-until-the-bar-closes real.

You walk home alone every night down cindered alleys
to the barks of dogs who should know you by now,
under stars bobbing in sultry air, barely glancing
at those windows, open to the breeze, where curtains
flutter like white moths and all the wives
in sleek slips toss and turn and stir in their sleep.

Electrifying Thoughts

If we could see our own neurons flash,
we would wave our arms at concerts
and *become* the light show.

When we plucked a petal from a flower,
we would see lightning stroke
down our hand, fork into our fingers
to set the petal aglow.

We could close our eyes as we kissed
but still see a reddened flirtation
of passion play back and forth between us
as if we were fireflies in June fields.

If we could see our own neurons flash,
we could read by our own flickering light;
it would brighten the pages as plots thickened,
dance like candlelight as metaphors
made our synapses fire in synchrony.

We'd be meteor showers. We'd
be each other's very own auroras.

For Billie Holiday

On her hundredth birthday, April 7, 2015

Smoke, shadowed mirror, gardenia at your ear.
Good Morning Heartache. Play the part. Shake
your head, smile a bit, for a while, and when it all
seems too much, a tear, a touch. Oh, Lester's sax!
Throw your head back, purl the words, pearl
the words, swirl the words, give the world the words.
Left with no choice, your burdened voice,
your needled arm, your dark-eyed charm.
"Strange fruit hangin' from poplar trees..."
"Use the alley door, if you please!"

Sandhill Seasons

Spring: Courtly Dancers

Sandhill cranes would never deign to dance
to Britten's piece from *Gloriana*
however glorious they might consider spring,
however much they might resemble
Renaissance dandies in tights and trunk-hose,
for they dance wings-akimbo, more akin
to jesters than knights, bound up
out of fields of grass, call their own rhythm,
bend and bow, skinny legs incongruous
beneath the mass of body, awkward hops
giving no insight into how they will soon
waltz away into that wilderness of sky.

Autumn: September Sonata

As September leans into October
cranes mount the air, watch the world
take on a Technicolor cast as they go.
Their calls more chortle than challenge,
their aims avocational now, no longer
charged with the urgency of spring.
They jaunt southward, jigging, jagged lines
of birds, legs trailing, necks leading,
and those wings, that take up so much
of the sky, wave to the awestruck world
as they fly.

Angel Ordering the Exiles from Paradise

After Karen Laub-Novak's painting,
"Exiles from Paradise"

They would become like rabbits
now. He knew he would soon
find them sneaking back into
the garden, lusting after sweet
berries, succulent pears, jewel-
brilliant pomegranate seeds.

They would couple like rabbits,
too; their offspring would be
as devoted to poaching as the
damned pair, the man, his rib-
wife. Naked, lacking feathers,
fur, they had daubed themselves
with clays and stains, covered
their bodies in vain attempts
to mimic better beings.

But they could not blend in.
He had them pegged,
knew their deceits before they
could fully form their plans.
They would soon weave cloaks,
he thought. And what poor imitations
of an angel's rainbow wings
those would be.

Invitation

Be my *Hi-Bred Pioneer* Princess,
my Empress *DeKalb*, my *Yield-
guard Triple Roundup-Ready* Duchess,
 my *Golden Harvest* Lady-In-Waiting.

I'll weave you a tassel wreath,
shower golden pollen in your path.
You'll be slender and tall as a hybrid stalk,
bright and shining and sheathed in green,
graceful as corn silk in the breeze.

Come run the rows, whip back the husks,
bite into the sweet crunching kernels.

Be my Grundy County 197-Bushel-
Per-Acre Beauty, my Queen of Corn.

Emily Baking

I wonder if
her house-dress
was white as flour,
if she jotted
lines of poetry
by wiping her finger
through the dusted table,
if the dough rose like the images
in her head, if her recipe
books had stanzas scribbled
on the margins, verse
with meter measured
as accurately as
ingredients, if exotic
words came smelling
of coconut, if the
heated glow of the stove
had her wiping her brow
with her apron, slant
rhymes already swirling
behind her eyes like
batter, butter smooth.

—After a National Public Radio piece on an Emily Dickinson recipe
for coconut cake.

Bly's Cows

"... the wind
Blowing across the rumps of grazing cows."
- Robert Bly, "Like the New Moon, I Will Live My Life"

When Robert Bly wrote of cows
he anchored the earth with them,
let them tell us the wind's direction,
had them quietly snort their expectations.
The world moved around them unnoticed.

His cows could never imagine how
we chew our worries like cud,
how we bite off expectations
at the nub like grass overgrazed,
leave the ground beneath us
windblown, overexposed.

"Thirty or so Black Angus hold down their earth
Among silvery grasses blown back and forth in
the wind."
- Robert Bly, "Living a Week Alone"

Grasses glisten, glide on wind,
surf with eddies. Each blade
knows its sole purpose today:
accentuate the stolid; outline
these black blobs of beeves; serve
as footlight-flooded stage; count
off split seconds for those who
do not choose to move.

The Intrinsic Essence of Hay

"... the cows ... caring nothing for all this,
Their noses in incense hay..."
- Robert Bly, "A Walk"

Sun-warmed scent of hay rolls in fields,
the moist center still on its way

to drying: alfalfa, brome, bluestem,
switchgrass, lespedeza. The cows

sniff, lift their heads a bit, compare
notes on aromas: protein stewing

in the bright day, cut stems still
oozing sap, green chlorophyll giving

way to amber, then gold. Their stomachs
rumble; their rumens run riot.

Jacob's Angels

"And he dreamed, and behold a ladder
set up on the earth, and the top of it
reached to heaven: and behold the angels
of God ascending and descending on it."
—Genesis 28:12 (King James Version)

Angel circus act? What else would
he dream on the way from Beersheba?
Maybe it was some bad well water?
Or the Negev heat? The rocks for pillows?
But there they were: angel acrobats (easy,
with wings), gymnasts (wings as balance
beams), contortionists (wings a definite
disadvantage).

If you think a lot of them fit on the head
of a pin, just imagine loading a ladder
with cherubim (chorists), seraphim
(spotlights), archangelistas (all dolled
up like Ziegfeld girls), one per rung,
others hovering about, traffic jam of them.
All excusing themselves. "Pardon." "So
sorry." "A bit busy today, eh?" "Gets worse
as you go higher."

Jacob, suddenly sitting up, rubbing
at the sleep in his eyes, shaking his head,
while, in the back-ground, angels are tugging
on that ladder, gesticulating, giggling,
and Jacob looks up just a second too late
to see the last rung sliding up, up,
up into the cumulus.

Leaving Delhi for Nagpur

They stare innocently
through the windows

of closed cars, foreheads
stroked vertically for Vishnu,

horizontally in triplets for Shiva, men
with dark eyes, white beards, women

with red dots and ebony hair, not
one embarrassed by open curiosity.

They pass by our view as individual
faces, become all a blur as the train

picks up speed, as it rattles toward
Delhi's troubled boundaries, passes

houses being built in layers, room by
room, hovels, shacks of stacked panels,

corrugated rust, and then, in open
fields, the morning squat of women,

their bright saris flowers
lit by sun.

The Couple Who Once Lived on this Farm

We didn't know them, what they
looked like, what they said into each
other's ears as moonlight's quadrangle
morphed its way across the bedroom
floor, what she thought as she stared
through the steam, poured the boiling
water off ears of corn or small, red
potatoes, how he scraped mud and
manure off his boot heels every time
he came to the door, the sound grating
or pleasing, depending on their moods.

Perhaps we can learn from the dust
on that sill. Purse our lips, blow up
a cloud of particles, the thick harvest
of years, the accumulation of dandruff
and skin cells, talcum, the dried
crumbs of biscuits, pollen from mullein,
from corn, from blue coneflowers.
We might sniff something in that dust,
sneeze, develop antibodies for specific
things we never suspected, never
imagined that we could ever, all
these years later, come to know about
the two of them.

Love's Last Letter

dark confetti of starlings
  murmuring across morning's
    dead-eyed mosaic sky

then these words
  inked across a page
    as if in flight

this nib issuing
  a ribbon of black
    that twists back and forth

binding a heart's
  fragmented clottings
    between loops and curls

meandering
  past emotions too fragile
    to be named

trailing off like love
  gone hollow as the bones
    of birds

IED/PTSD

Your friends' eyes blink worry-line codes,
navigate glances laden with dark alleys.

They proffer bitter advice spiced
with apologies, reach for your hand, but

it has become a trigger with wires wending
into your heart, a timer that sets them

to trembling with each click. They ache
to know which colored coil they need to cut,

which profession of love might ground
the uncertain and secret circuits of your soul.

Forbidden Fruit

1

Tears were shed in Eden over mangos, I'd wager—certainly not for mundane apples. There was sun enough, water enough for tropical fare—else, why call it *Paradiso*? That snide snake would never have caught Eve off balance or suckered Adam, stumbling in his bare feet, with some crisp white pome fruit, ruby peel or not. Nectared honey-flesh and gold-blushed green-orange skin it would have been that slushed juice and pulp over their tongues as they bit at the bait.

2

Haunted to this day, we lost souls seek out statues in the naves of chapels, squint at plaques telling us their saints' names, catalog each one's special grace, each one's particular blessings. We plead for intercession, all the while recalling how the forked tongue flicked, licked the sweet liquid that lingered on our mango-moistened lips.

3

To test for ripeness, you must hold a mango using just the tips of your fingers, thumb opposed to the four (why else would God have granted us such a boon?). Apply light pressure. Palpate. Feel for a springing beneath the yielding. No squishing, no holding firm, just enough of an elastic sort of softness. For perfection this ripe, you, too, would have embraced the burden of original sin. Admit it. Even now, your body gives you away: The flush of saliva from under your tongue. Saliva drenching your soft palate, glistening the silken inner linings of your mangoed cheeks.

Newly Released, Classified

Just as we cannot see
redacted words, so they
cannot see, or talk, to us.

They are blindfolded,
gagged; they can barely
breathe, the black marker ink
brings tears to their eyes.

They are becoming frantic,
asking "Why?" and we,
reaching toward the disconnected,
innocent, inane words peering out at us
from between the black slashes,
cannot answer.

The prodigal son goes to the disco

all blurry-eyed, Quaalude-floppy legs,
"That's the way I like it!" she chants,
pulls him over, crumples his polyester
jacket, pats his breast pocket for a packet
of pills, a roll of bills, crooks a finger
through his gold chain, leads him
out onto the floor, the mirrored shards
pimping out flashes of color, the bass
ringing in his ears. He hasn't seen
daylight much less sunlight for weeks,
his half of his old man's fortune down,
now, to small bills and coins.

The blonde's interest is already
drifting off toward another pimply-
faced kid fresh off the caravan from
the Negev. She turns to the girl child
she's training up, says "Don't feel bad,
for him, my pomegranate, my hennaed-
lamb—it's their sons those old bastards
welcome back with open arms. It's
their damn sons that they forgive."

—Thanks to Jeanette Powers for the prompt,
"The prodigal son goes to the disco."

"Acting is behaving truthfully under **imaginary circumstances.**"

~ Sanford Meisner

Ways of the Wind

"There she was
In her yellow dress
And her hair open to adventure..."
—Xanath Caraza, from her poem
"Matilde en la Hamaca"

The wind had its way with her hair—
made it flow and twist, turned
its movements liquid, its strands
currents of streams braiding
the valley of the Brahmaputra.

The wind had its way with her hair—
brushed it with bergamot oils
from Calabria, bathed it in the moist
breaths of benedictions, prayers
for intercession mouthed by processions
of faithful in the plaza *Catedral Basílica*
de la Virgen de la Asunción.

The wind had its way with her hair—
used it, strand by strand, to catch
all the hues of a Sinai sunset,
as if it were yarn carded
for a coat of many colors.

The wind had its way with her hair—
sent it searching the leniency
of her neck, the Sahara slopes of
her shoulders, had it conform
to its caresses, its advances, its
countless ways with love.

Birdsong

"... the upside down song
a bird sings, flying past, reflected in the water."
—William Stafford, from the
poem "Old Ways, New Ways."

You know you have perfect pitch
when you can transcribe
the brown thrasher's morning song
onto staff paper, accidentals and
slur marks and flagged notes
bounding across the page. They flow
into your ears and out your fingers
without a blotch of ink, without
an error as you paint the theme
onto paper, capture the variations
measure after measure, the secret
code of notated music as brilliant
on the page, in its own way, as
the bird's song rarifying the air,
then compressing it, carrying waves
of trills into the depths of your inner ear,
that French horn in reverse, sending
your auditory nerves an orgasm
of sound that reverberates the halls
of your brain, whips the neurons that
control your fingers, pins down, in
all its intricacy, the intensity
of being this one, singular,
sunlit, morning bird.

Ante Meridiem

The unexpected clarity
of this frigid morning:
less than half a moon,

stars that stab right through
the slab of sky. Low clouds
huff back the light, flock

the black with luminous gray
humps. My breath puffs
out, a small replication.

The dog noses through
frost-fringed leaves for what
moulders beneath the crust

of cold. Small meanings
and parallels and the earth
prodding us back into

the slack dawn of its
repetition. We pair
of old recidivists

persevere, plod, plot
the day's recurring
necessities.

—for our Labrador Retrievers: Misha, Joe, and Jenna

God rode by

on his bicycle today.
It was painted red, a rich shade,
redolent of Baroque oils,
reminiscent of the candle-
lit cloth of de la Tour's
Penitent Magdalene.

"Nice paint job!" I called.
"Thanks!" He yelled back.
"Can't stop now.
Maybe later."

He turned, noticed
the pothole in the road,
swerved around it with
a certain grace
I could only describe
as Divine.

Wide-Eyed Walker

Barefoot walk on cold floors—
Strange the paths you turn to take—
Opening the closed doors,
Sleepwalking yourself awake.

Strange the paths you turn to take—
Are you dreaming as you pace?
Sleepwalking yourself awake—
I see no answer in your face.

Are you dreaming as you pace?
Open eyes, what do you see?
I see no answer in your face—
Do you remember me?

Open eyes, what do you see,
Barefoot on the cold floors?
Do you remember me
Opening the closed doors?

—Thanks to Jeanette Powers for the prompt,
"sleepwalking yourself awake"

What Beauty Is For

*"And have you too finally figured
out what beauty is for?"*
—Mary Oliver

For getting on in the world;
for holding up the sky;
for covering iniquity with brilliance;

for all the things that glance off
our peripheral vision but stay relevant;
for all the times we failed;

for mapping the intricacies of souls;
for children still learning the nature of things;
for a glimpse of what we wish eternity to become.

Renaissance

The sun in winter fancies itself medievalist,
projects shadows of frost-shattered asters,
arabesques them onto curled leaves. Baroque
in its intentions, it patterns chaotic *fleur de lys*,
damascenes twigs; pebbles become rime-silvered
objets d'art, interwoven grass and bits of leaf
appear torn from hand loomed tapestries, now
Norman, now Flemish, now Moorish. We watch
it indulge each Januaried pretension.

Moon Series

1

Early in the tenth month
the moon's arc sits on
the horizon for just an
instant, and you know
you could set it to rocking
with a nudge, a tap.
Go ahead. Touch the cusp.
Slide your index finger's
pad along that sickle-
edge, let it ride the ridges
of your skin, ping
against the tip of your
nail. Twang it. Listen
for the high-pitched
vibration of that curl
of light, catch the slight
rumble as the craters
crunch against the edge
of the earth, the brilliant
rolling arc weighed down
by the dark and intricately
textured sphere it holds
so close.

2

Scatter the blue with droplets,
with particles of particular-size.
Tinge the sun's light to terra cotta;
to the orange of leaves whose
chlorophyll has faded;
the carotene of fall; the red
of iron, oxidized; the carmine of
cochineal. Flush that altered
light across the pocked surface
of the moon, the shaded lunar
luminance blushing the red
of hemoglobin-laden capillaries.
Behold, the blooded but
bloodless moon.

The journalism of opium

never mentions red fields
of poppies scalding through
the valley haze – life's blood
pooling the misty passages
between Afghan foothills.

A rooster might crow
beside a hut, the scent
of mint waft from a dish of lamb,
the icy fields that feed streams
might streak stony slopes
in glinting patterns.

All we read of are junkies
like zombies stumbling
into tenement nights
searching for the next billow
of Badakhshan snow.

Forgiveness

grinds grit and bile into a slurry
of slip, into silky wet clay.
Forgiveness turns cold earth
on a spindle, forms it with
the warm friction of your
fingers into a hollow crock
for storing spite.

Forgiveness watches as you
set a lid in place, stretches
as you push the glazed jar
across the floor into that
far corner where offenses
and rancor are set to fade
and shrink away.

Forgiveness wipes your
hands clean with a homespun
apron, sets you to climbing
steps to return to the sun.

Mayflies Rise

*"... one Mayfly's day holds
one eternity."*
—Mark Zelman, from his poem,
"I Could Say"

Mayflies rise from water
like mist, mark the still
air's breath with long thread-tails,
kite and drop and dodge
and dance the day's delirium.

The gold-foiled water, dappled
where they left diver's suits of crumpled skin,
mirrors their flight in circular intersections,
captures, in the Mayflies' lifting,
their eternally vanishing reflections.

Glacial Debris

Having traversed wet morning shadows
to get to the boulder, she dripped
dark grey spots from an ankle,
watered a crusty patch of lichen
with a toe.

Lying back, she matched
the curvature of her spine
to the granite, stretched until
all thirty-three vertebrae
were pressed tightly
to the surface of the rock.

Closing her eyes
to the sky, she shivered,
wondered why
the topography of her body
did not conform as well
to his contours
as to those of this cold,
this dead stone.

Four Old Barns

The Barn as Lecture: a tome on the philosophical
underpinnings of character and ethical fortitude,
its cosmetics appalling, decrepit of face and
skin, splintered and scarred, ripped and riven.
We notice what is gone, what has been taken
of grace and spare beauty, and thus miss
the straight and unwavering roof, the solid,
secure trusses, the un-sagging corrugations of
the *casque chapeau*, the unflagging ridge line,
the rafters and joists, purlins and under-purlins,
the whole stalwart basis of being a barn.

> *February Barn* hunches its shoulders
> up around its ears, still can't get warm,
> opens its mouth to moan, watches
> sunlight creep down tree branches,
> would give a lurch to lift itself into
> that warmth if it could. Instead, just
> creaks, wheezes wind through splits
> in its siding, it's face gray as frostbite.

The Angularity Barn boasts obtuse corners,
patterns of weathered wood, horizontal
boards, vertical ones, acute geometry and
jagged polygons that jab and poke at
nature's amorphous, rolling fluff, at her
indeterminateness, all the while losing,
drib by drab, its inherent order, its nailed
hardiness, its measured tangents to the
incremental creep of time, the mindless
random emptiness of entropy.

Meeting heading-seas of green bow-on
day after day eventually leads to this:
Barn Adrift in ripening grain, doldrums
of golden swells, bobbing balloons of clouds,
haze marking the wakes of hull-up
combines, the placid form of a hipped-gambrel
roof, all headway squandered. Time alone
knows how and when to expect
the quartering winds, the beam-on waves
of wheat, the finality of broaching-to.

Pretense

The new knife is a serrated,
heavy razor. He allows its heft
to carry it through the ripe
tomato, uses his hand merely
as a pivot, a fulcrum, a
turning point, just the way he allows
life to happen, events to drop
into place, with never a thumbs-up,
thumbs down, with never a push,
a nudge from him, never a lean
to left or right, a raised eyebrow.
a nod, an inclined or tilted head.

He imagines letting the knife ride
on the corrugated tendons of
his wrist, drawing it across,
watching it wobble up and down
over gristle, blue veins, imagines
it slicing, each serration sinking
lower, viscous blood leaking
onto the cutting board, slowly
dissolving into the tomato's
watery leavings. He wouldn't
need to push down at all, he
thinks. This weight, alone,
would suffice.

Cerebellum's Fire:

The bold but dim-browed ancestor of ours
who first gathered up in glowing embers
lightning's gift to man to light the hours—
the first true man none of us remembers.

    The sight of Mongol ponies, wild and free,
    sweeping, massed, across the wind-blown plains,
    the dream of warriors following his lead,
    that sparked Genghis Khan's ambitious brain.

From the crucible of Isaac Newton's mind,
revealed, from alchemy's dim and gloomy gleams,
the way God's planetary gears toil and grind,
bare and bold, and not the mystery it seemed.

    From a body pinned in place by ALS,
    in Hawking's mind the bright universe expands—
    this man who is all but motionless
    sees how the world was born and how it ends.

Dragonflier

Because you crawled from dim, watery depths
to conquer the luminous sky, I seek insight.
With surgical scrutiny I search for secrets hidden
in the intricate folds and angles of your cut-glass wings.

These scimitar blades flashed, thrust, parried with
whirling vortices of air, propelled your zooming,
darting, dazzling gyrations. Gyrations that should
have brought applause. "Bravo!" "Encore!"

Gyrations that did bring breathless wonder to me,
grounded observer, open-mouthed watcher, earth-
bound plodder, pitifully envious would-be Daedalus.

Gyrations that brought my jealous net swinging
to pluck you from the glorious sky. You were stunned,
indignant, but knew that, having captured you,
I had not captured your soul.

Now I peer through the varied panes
of your window wings, panes transparent,
panes translucent, panes opaque, smoked-
glass panes with a peek-hole rubbed clear
in the center between the mullion veins.

But the view is blurred. The secrets are filtered,
absorbed, refracted, held within. Millennia of secrets
that grace your too-few days with this marvelous gift.

Your incomparable mastery of the barely-tangible air
will take more divining than I have time for today.
Perhaps more divining than is mine to possess.

Refugee Shores

> *"Rumor, the swiftest plague there is, went straight out*
> *To all the settlements of Libya."*
> *—Sarah Ruden's Translation of Vergil's*
> *"The Aeneid" (Book 4: 173-174)*

Packed tighter than the slave ships
that once plied these shores,
fishing boats with un-caulked seams
and hulls soft with rot push off from
the beach, people layered in holds,
sitting shoulder to shoulder, gunwale
to gunwale. Assured that Italy is only
hours away, they hear rumors of Europe
swishing in on the waves, watch hope
tread water in each other's eyes.

—For the Mediterranean refugees of
the 2nd decade of the 21st Century.

"Acting is in **everything but the words.**"
~ Stella Adler

Sweet, Your Heart

Sweet, your heart, that clenches,
that pressurizes the systole of it all,
the hydraulic purpose of your life,
the thrumming foundation of your
most basic rhythm: its quenching
shushings, its whump-a-whump
rappings against the rib-slatted
confines of your thorax, the way
the flesh of you damps those
pulsations, the way the tangle
of blood vessel branchings
ramble their way through you,
the ramrod peaks that balloon
your arterial walls only to dissipate
into capillary whispers, the curious
contortions of your erythrocytes,
the way they swell their dimpled way
to the nether network where artery
fingertips stretch and reach for those
of veins. From the pumping thumping
engine room of your chest to the soft,
insistent tap tappata tap tappata tap
at your wrist, at your temple, the blue
roadways of heart messages mapped
onto the parchment world of your skin:
You, sweet. Your heart.

Cowley County October

Virginia Creeper spatters
the hackberries along Grouse Creek
with splashes the same rusty
color as the old man of a pump jack
up on the crest of the hill.

The cloisonné face of a cock pheasant
slips between bronzed shafts of bluestem.

A plume of dust chases a pickup
but can't follow it over the bridge.
The smell of parched leaves drifts
through the golden tracery
of cottonwood trees.

At the pool below the run,
abstract impressionist carp
swirl temporary images
of distant spiral galaxies
onto the surface of the creek.

Ink Blots and Wax Seals

Once you would have placed your thoughts
down as they came, no highlight and delete,
no cut and paste, just dark and stark cursive
script against pale paper.
Oh, an occasional line-through,
a careless smudge, a drop of ink that
dripped from quill or pen, then was
blotted, but words by and large
sequenced as they were formed
in the wrinkled kernel of your mind,
rearranged, if at all, during a pause,
pen pensive for a short while, a quizzical
look crossing your brow, perhaps,
but for just the briefest time,
for the ink was drying at the nib,
so you had to get to it quickly—
to the nubbin of what you had
to say, and it had to flow, the pen
lifting only at the end of a word,
the letters connected, thus making
each word something more of a unit,
a thing, a being in its own right;
each sentence, then, a family,
the words related to each other
by the meaning you endowed them with
as you formed your message, your thoughts,
your warm regards, your
urgent passion, your nuggets
of truth, the emotions you folded,
closed, entrusted to a drop of wax
and to a signet seal.

The Mystery of Disappearing Bees

Missing bees are hollows of air surrounding
flowers with swarms of regret.

Pollen is wasting away like poetry
written in forgotten languages.

Where is the wage of the summer's toil—
the syrup of nectars distilled in the furnaces
of dancing bees?

And why do these empty hexagons
hold only the stark geometry
of absence?

Reading *Moby Dick* Again

"... a way I have of driving off the spleen,"

says Ishmael, and I wonder
if the writing of it is as much the remedy
as the decoction of travel, the pen and page
as much as the Pequod-prescription,
if the narrative, as dense as a cud of bolus,
is truly the *prima medicina* for a man of the sea?
At least for the sailing man of letters who longs
to be shut of the shore, carpet bag stuffed
with shirts, paper, a bottle of India's finest,
black, corked, ready.

"The whale would by all hands
be considered a noble dish,
were there not so much of him"

... and *Moby Dick* a noble book, perhaps
because there is so much of him,
and all that explanatory digression
between the true and hearty, grab you
by the short-hairs-narration is really needed.
Because, by Ahab, by Queequeg, by God,
you cannot appreciate the story
without you understand the job:
the whaler's lot in life, his devotion
to his brothers at sea, to that noble beast,
his prey, the whale, the incarnation
of his every need, his very nature.

Summer

Trees gone mad
with chloroplasts
toss leaves
into the sky,
billow explosions
of leaves, launch

them into summer
air, waft them through
open expanses, trade
oxygen for CO_2, make
themselves giddy with it.

Their sugary
sap spirals down
tunnels of phloem,
their roots tighten
into the earth,
hold on for dear life.

Dry Eyes

In times of drought
you don't waste tears.
When clouds that should
stretch overhead
march, instead,
in parade a mile
or more away,
when columns of rain—
gray-cloaked clergy in procession—
solemnly dispense their blessings
out beyond the county line,
you must stay dry-eyed,
even when they don't
turn their heads, even
when they don't so much
as nod your way
as they pass.

tree shadows
       angle
    their skeletal souls
     like Chinese
     script,
  henggou
      strokes
against   roof lines,
   na   inked   at mansards
    shuzhe on the dormers bow
                formally,
      and sit,
        knees bent,
   leaning,   their
      backs to the sun

Morels

Morchella lift convoluted intentions
on stems clean and hollow as bird bones,
make mazes for May's aradids, scrunch
gnomed caps up through their elm leaf-
littered forest haunts, peeking, furtive,

while

we search, big-eyed, compare what we
see among ground debris with patterns
impressed on the complex paths of our
brains, correlate ridges, pits, wrinkled
edges, shapes recalled from April dreams.

Roy J. Beckemeyer

Insinuation

"The wind is all innuendo..."
- Kathleen Wakefield,
from her poem, "Afterward"

Today the wind
veils its truths
in leaves' allusions:
in their sly sidewise
glances, in the
faces they hide
behind each
others' fan-like
tilts and twists,
each-others'
geisha-guile.

Alaskan Food Chain

Perhaps we should have sympathized.
The wheezing caribou,
rib cage heaving,
looked back in mid-stride.
Terror exposed
the white of her eyes.

But after all, we're predators, too,
and are not immune
to the fever of running wolves.

Certainly, bounding over
spruce-shadowed drifts,
tracking the tense
odor of caribou,
held more appeal
than empathizing
with a hamstrung cow,
already sinking,
in shock and submission,
into the snow.

Besides, her rapidly clouding eyes
never saw
the blood-soaked muzzles
of the wolves,
never saw the brutal darkness
that lingered, terribly,
on your face,
and on mine.

Corvus vesperus

> *"I watched them as they stropped their beaks*
> *against the bark, their blue-black glinted eyes*
> *upon me."—Paul Mariani, from his poem,*
> *"The Eastern Point Meditations."*

Crows cant across
the leaden evening,
a blitz of black,
careening, cawing,
their scattered course
consistent enough
to rut the sky.

They drop, by some sign
prearranged, settle
into tangled trees
along the street:
raucous crew, blotches
of black, blatant caws,
ebony cloaks.

Winter-stoic branches
bend, creak
as crows shift, shuffle,
shutter their wings:
lamp black clumps,
sable standards, banners
dark as midnight,
stark hearts of grief.

Meanings:

Acedia \a-sə -'dē-ə \:   ~ *spiritual torpor; apathy*

Lead-lidded eyes, mouth a chasm
behind cupped hand, head-bowed
willow-hair, shoulders slumped
like the leeward slope of a dune,
soul leaking through the soles
of feet, spirit footsteps vaporizing,
leaving no sign for any rare or random
stranger who might even deign to care.

Clarty \'klɑr: tɪ \   ~ *bedaubed with sticky dirt*

Soil between nails and fingers
arc each digit with black grime.
Whorls on finger pads stained
by damp earth; sweat streaked
with dust turned to salty mud
enriched with skin cells.

Organic with the remnants of each
phylum, each class, each order of life,
wet soil inks us all with the stuff
of geology, of biology, of being.

Eidetic \ī'detik\   ~ *extraordinarily accurate and vivid recall*

To have stored everything that ever lit
the fuse end of your optic nerves, that
wiggled the hairs on your basilar membrane,
that pushed your somato-sensory buttons,
tickled your tongue's papillae, basted
bitterness against G-protein coupled receptors.
To have assigned each sense a number,
a Dewey Decimal, a Library of Congress,
a Retrieval Code of Your Own Devising.
And you, standing at the end of the endless
row of stacks, watch them dim to paleness
in the distance, and recede, recede, recede.

Effulgence \i-'fʊl-jǝn(t)s\ ~ *radiant splendor; brilliance*

Light, not wave or particle,
but a wash of brightness, a
splash of lumens, photons
floating free. Drowning all day in a sea
of light, gulping it down with
each blink, each squint, each
focused, equal-pupil stare.

Flint: \'flint\ ~ *variety of hard quartz that breaks*
with a sharp edge

Conchoidal quartz sharp
enough to shave hairs, slit
throats, pass through hide
and muscle, knapped with
fingernail-shaped absences
that leave edges hard and thin
as something honed.

Piercer of life forms, arbiter
of soul releases, earth-forged
crystal accidently discovered
beneath some biped's suddenly
sliced plantar fascia. Adopted
and adapted tool of the ancients,
even then older than flesh, older
than death, the age of stone itself.

Gnathic \'na-thik\ ~ *of or relating to the jaw*

Hinged, articulated, set about
with molars, incisors, grinders
of grain, breakers of bones,
enameled compression crunchers.
Opener of yawns, of O-mouthed
screams, entryway for dental drills
and scrapers, means by which
snapping turtles hold on for dear life.
Hard G's, when lost to nasal N's, gnaw
at us, sit there in silence, all bent over,
grouchy, geared to growl.

This Poetry

Shakespeare's sonnets, perfect, sublime—
this tortured rhyme.

The thousands of years Homer thrives—
our too-short lives.

Literature's long probity—
this poetry.

The bards and we—a coterie:
their classics with their long-armed reach—
these stutters of our modern speech.
This tortured rhyme, our too-short lives: This poetry.

—*This poem is in a Spanish form called the* Ovijello.

Weather Words

Two degrees of separation
and isobars of constant genetics
delineate the here-born high from
the there-born low, the stratus-
brained from the cumulonimbi,
and all we hold up front
are the cyclonic winds of *we*
and *they*, the soggy depths
of indeterminate and unpredictable
relationships, our high friends,
our low enemies, and the storm fronts
we invent, and then must learn
to weather.

August Sees Signs of September

Goldenrod will soon spark the dark green alleys
like sunlight speckling a forest floor.
Then sumac leaves will bleed out from under
chlorophyll, drip from branches to the ground.
Grass seed heads will turn silvery gray, aged
a lifetime since green-sprigged spring.
Cicadas are already shifting into low gear, grinding
and double clutching their way to silence.
Tree leaves, nodding in the rising wind, tug at petioles,
test for a slackness, for any sign of weakness at the stem.

Early Onset

When beta amyloid and tau plaque
tangle process and transmission
in your brain,
will I fade as well?

Will my face, my voice, the feel
of my hand holding yours spark
less brightly in the darkening
halls of your cortex?

If I am what you remember:
when your neurons no longer know
the secret recipe for acetylcholine,
will I still exist?

"Death is just **the last scene of the last act.**"
~ Joyce Carol Oates

Missing

The prairie possesses no cataracts,
no water plunging toward mist, no rocky
promontories sluiced by green plumes
of streaming water, just wide, mud-choked valleys,
flood plain inundations, sand and silt-bound
creamed-coffee in spate careening past bridge
piers, spinning into sucking vortices
that pull, and, spiteful, keep what they pull
down into fluid thick as paint, that only
release what they now own a week later:
mud-laden, torn, clasped by the roots
of a torrent-borne tree a half-mile
downstream, swinging lazily, face-down in
the wide, gentler eddies of the waning flood.

Melancholia: Class Photograph, 1948

"The old props vanish
By which we posed"
- Mark Strand

They stand quietly—props in a warehouse,
arrayed in rows. Their forgotten faces,
open, innocent of guile, serve to rouse
faint glimmers of simpler times, past places,

details I strive so hard to remember.
Children once removed, it seems I and they
now share this bitter harvest: a slender
stock of years remains, each frail, tattered, frayed.

Never knowing the number exactly,
we prefer to see ourselves as we were.
Unwilling to face the bitter facts, we
now, as in our youth, turn away, defer

those thoughts of coming things, of tomorrow's
dwindling years, future's surfeit of sorrows.

Blessings

—for Pat

Your mother's hair, your father's nose,
the bedroom eyes your own,
the whispered words that could fill tomes,
the hands my hands enclose.

The back you turned, but not for long,
the tears that stained the floor,
the times when I, lost and unmoored,
admitted I was wrong.

The ways you changed that never seemed
to change the one you are.
This life foreseen, from off so far,
we made real from our dreams.

Under Prairie Skies

We make daily withdrawals from
our allocations of heartbreak, hail storms,
stillborn children, sit staring at
the Spartan silence of burial plots,

remember grandfathers who spent
their days wresting land from the prairie,
acre by acre, who claimed it
with hedge rows, section lines,

cemeteries, dream that our children,
building lives on these difficult bones,
will lift their eyes to that far horizon
where stars and earth collide.

Amplification

"My father could hear a little animal step,
or a moth in the dark against the screen..."
- William Stafford, from his poem, "Listening"

To hear her heart beat
requires a certain intimacy,
but at an impersonal remove—
filtered through the cold
bell of the stethoscope.

Her heart sounds are amplified,
a shushing rhythm of seas pounding
shores; his hand is so still,
not rustling, his curled fingers
resting quietly against her skin.

He listens for something more,
some cross current of interference,
some odd, off, beat. He travels
the shores of her chest, listening.

The cold center of the scope
is a bulls-eye that draws her body's
heat. Her heart shoves blood
in pulses, fills capillaries, brings
warmth, along with all that sound,
to that spot, that locus of cold logic
and centered hearing.

All she can hear is his
quiet, steady breathing.

She listens for a quick intake of air,
a held breath, a sigh, some small
sound that will tell her he has found
whatever it is he listens for.

Winter's Weft

As we stitch these days into the garland
of time that binds us to this hallowed place,
as we search for patterns in this far stand
of wind-woven grasses, the prairie's lace,

as we draw from our allotment of tears
and wind-chills and storms and snow-splattered sky,
as we use each other to allay our fears,
and brace, one against the other, to get by,

let us look up and find that calm North Star,
the world's pivot about which we all whirl.
We'll watch stars rise and fall, some near, some far,
and listen as coyotes wail and skirl,

and weave this winter, as the night air clears,
into the wreath of our apportioned years.

Rosarium Threnody

"Tell the beads
of the chromosomes
like a rosary, Father."
—Kathryn Kysar from her poem,
"Coyote Addresses Science"

We grasp the string of chromosomes
like prayer beads, follow, finger
by finger, the coiled helix home,

count mitochondria for the mother
of God. We bear each mutation
to the cross as if we trail another

time to Golgotha. Your faulty
genes, my distorted DNA, bad
seed or ovum, no matter, only

the twisted proteins, the blood
slow to clot, the child, small as
my hand, too soon in the world.

Five times tenfold, here at the tomb,
"blessed is the fruit of thy womb."

—for Loretta Marie and Roy Stanley
Beckemeyer and for Mary (9-14-1942)

Armadillos

along the highway
lie, small heaps
enclosed in light
armor, leathery, still,
in their rigor-rigged
pose, legs pegged out
so abruptly we
can imagine their eyes
as comic book x's.

Placed on their own
gelled blood, they
punctuate the miles,
each one a small ode
to that shuffling
life by which they abide,
ride out storms, cross,
at last, into the finality
wrought of macadam
roads.

And our quick glance
back into the rear view
mirror—the only blessing
we seem able to bestow.

Aubade in Four Parts

1   Dawn clicks into place
    like another gear-tooth advancing
    toward the end of days, makes
    an escapement snick
    as clock-spring proteins
    harden into coils, into knots
    bound by enzymes
    set on edge by light.

2   The edge of light shoulders
    its way under the sill of stars
    burgles yet another night,
    tucks it away, strikes its
    notebook page with a slash,
    the empty pages fewer,
    now, the binding loose,
    looser, loosening.

3   All across the eastern horizon
    watchers stare at each other's
    silhouettes, shove armloads
    of light past themselves until
    the photons flow in spates,
    wash over their ankles,
    their knees, splash their faces
    with a certain knowledge
    of contour, of color.

4   The old shell game, the quick shuffle;
    you can't keep track: the cups
    moved, palmed, the little
    ball there one instant, gone
    the next. Then, in the blur
    of shifting hands, the starlit
    night is folded into ever flatter
    layers until the paper chrysanthemum
    of day suddenly pops
    into bloom.

Recalled After Reading a Jim Harrison Poem

I once saw a beetle
fall to the ground
as if shot, crack onto
the driveway, not just
stunned, but stilled
to finality, one second flying
through air-insubstantial,
the next gob-smacked
by a concrete slab
that might as well have been,
was, indeed, the whole
mass of the old Earth,
and thought to myself,
yes, that is what I have seen
in people, too, swimming
through life, crawl slowed
to back-stroke, perhaps,
but still gliding through
water, feeling it pass
alongside their bodies,
slithering, sliding, making
headway until they reach
the end of the pool,
simply unwilling to do
a final flip turn for even
one more lap.

Footage from Aleppo

"...a lark talking madness in some
corner of the sky." - Joseph Auslander,
from his poem "Dawn at the Rain's Edge."

Laser-eyed bombs
streak in, unheard
and unseen until
the earth, flash-
blinded by frenzy,
grabs the sky
by the throat,
shakes it, erupts,
roils up.

A flock of short-toed larks
takes flight at the madness,
sweeps over the roadside
in an aching cloud, a dancing
random swirl, its movements
mirrored, for just a moment,
by a dead man's *kaffiyeh*, blown
free, billowing: birds and scarf
a stark calligraphy, a sort
of script, a staging,
a new orthography
of atonement.

Quail Hunt

Clatter of quail wings
climbs the stairs of the sky;
my gun barrel tracks,
traces a wisp of feathery
contrail eddying in the wake
of that pattern, that
formation, that living
gestalt of grace,
the arching flight path
pulls gun and sightline
and breath cloud all
in one motion;
my sinews contract,
neurons fire on automatic
pilot, my long back muscles
do the complex ballet
of twisting, turning; those
small pectoral muscles
pulse, pull feather
shafts that slice air
and shove it spinning
into motion, but
the gunmetal tip
catches up, passes by
and the timing:
never a thought,
just action, action,
small muscles of hand
and finger connected
directly to these eyes.
Then the stock, cradled,
jolts back, and the great cracking
sound, sharp, violent,
contained, the burst,
the burst of down and
the tumbling, erratic
scramble of ebbing life
toward the arms of the earth.
The sound passes unheard
by the dying quail;

the whole *danse macabre*
ends in slow motion:
gun barrel and bird
on opposite paths at last,
 upward recoil and downward
plunge choreographed,
the grand play, the ferocious
play, the beauty and mystery
of the intertwining of my life
and this one small death,
now forever linked,
inseparable.

Leaning Westward

Sunrise stretching up behind us, the moon
    fading to a watermark in the backlit sky,
      we roll miles off I-70, watch rivers

go threadlike as the horizon expands into
    the flatness time has used to cap the Ogallala,

watch fields go from square to circular,
    cities wind down to scatterings of people spread
      here and there over the wide landscape, while

cattle, once dotted across vast pastures, crowd,
    shoulder to shoulder, into feedlot ghettos.

Plath's Children

"Perfection is terrible,
it cannot have children."
—Sylvia Plath

She closed the kitchen
in on herself with wet
cloths at door edges,
the children thus once
removed by doors,

once again by soggy
towels, the water oozing
from the weighty fabric
in shallow sheets across
the linoleum floor.

Morning Walk

Rain can't make up its
   misty-mind this morning.

List any kind of yawning,
   stretching dawning, and

you'd have it here. A song
   might ring out any day,

sunny or not, and anyway,
   that bright spot of a note

from the throat of a wren,
   or was it a sparrow, heard

through my ear's narrow filter
   could become, half-formed

though this train of thought
   might be, the most perfect

plum of a rainy-day refrain
   ever sung for me.

Prayer of Letting Go

Let me go to ground
   like the last aster
of November,

my eyes still looking
   upward, the first
winter snow outlining

the scaffolding of what
   has held me up through
this long season; let

the weight of that
   snow bring me gently
to my knees, to the earth

that helped build
   what remains here at
the end, the wind

whispering by to make
   my almost brittle
petals flare one last

time, their blue hearts
   blinking at the
ease of letting go.

Breathe

Soon enough,
your ribs
will encircle nothing
but fallow ground
impoverished of hearts,
will expand
and contract only
when the earth's clay
swells and shrinks.

Revel now
in the way
your lungs burnish
your blood to
a brighter red
and your heart opens
and closes like
a fist, grasping at
that brilliant stream,
sending it off in spurts
to engorge arteries,
to sate cells.

Place your faith in
staunch corpuscles,
reliably climbing their
blue way back toward
alveoli and air.

Inhale deeply.

Breathe.

Acknowledgments

I wrote some of these poems while participating in a closed Facebook group, *365 Poems in 365 Days*, a source of much inspiration and encouragement. My fellow *Wayward Poets* (in our ninth year of meeting weekly) continue to challenge me to meet their expectations; current members are Pat Beckemeyer, Dixie Brown, Judy Hatteberg, Susan Howell, Pat Latta, Melany Pearce, and Jane Ray. *Basement Bards* poetry critique-group members Pat Beckemeyer, Bob Dean, David Cook, Skyler Lovelace, and Diane Wahto have sharpened my writing with their perceptive comments. Pat Latta, Pat Beckemeyer, and Lindsey Martin-Bowen made comments on a draft manuscript. Finally, please note that the following poems first appeared elsewhere, some in a slightly altered form. I thank the editors of these venues for selecting them for publication:

"Alaskan Food Chain," *Gazebo*, 1977.
"Amplification" (as "Listening"), *I-70 Review*, 2017.
"Anderson Creek Creed," *Heartland! Poems of Love, Resistance, & Solidarity, 2018.*
"Angel Ordering Exiles from Paradise," *Psaltery & Lyre*, 2017.
"Annunciation Angel," *KYSO Flash*, 2018.
"Armadillos," *Poems-for-All*, #1521, 2017.
"August Sees Signs of September," *365 Days: A Poetry Anthology*, 365 Days Poetry, 2016.
"Bly's Cows," *I-70 Review*, 2016.
"Breathe," *River City Poetry*, Spring Issue 2018.
"Cerebellum's Fire," *Kansas Voices Anthology*; winner, 2016 *Kansas Voices Award.*
"*Corvus vesperus*" (as "Crows"), *365 Poems in 365 Days: A Poetry Anthology, Vol. 2.* 365 Days Poetry, 2018.
"Dragonflier," *ARGIA: The newsletter of the Dragonfly Society of the Americas*, 1997.
"Early Onset," *Wichita Broadside Project*, 2017, with art by Skyler Lovelace.
"Electrifying Thoughts," *The Midwest Quarterly*, 2014.
"Family," *River City Poetry*, Spring 2018 Issue.
"First Holy Communion," *Gimme Your Lunch Money: Heartland Poets Speak out against Bullies*, Paladin Contemporaries, 2016.
"Flint," *Flint Hills Review*, 2016.
"Footage from Aleppo," *Heartland! Poems of Love, Resistance, & Solidarity, 2018.*

"For Billie," *Gimme Your Lunch Money: Heartland Poets Speak out against Bullies,* Paladin Contemporaries, 2016.
"Glacial Debris," *Images: The Sunflower Literary Section,* 1978.
"Grain Elevator Gray," *Heartland! Poems of Love, Resistance, & Solidarity,* 2018.
"Great Blue Heron," *Zingara Poetry Review,* 2016.
"The Intrinsic Essence of Hay," *The Midwest Quarterly,* 2016.
"jack, 1941-1959," *Kansas City Voices,* 2014.
"Jacob's Angels," *The Ekphrastic Review, February 26,* 2016.
"Leaning Westward," *One Sentence Poems,* May 3, 2017.
"Mayflies Rise," *River City Poetry Summer Issue,* 2017.
"Meanings" (In part), *Titynope 'Zine,* 2017.
"Morning Walk" won the 2016 *Astra Arts Festival Poetry Award.*
"Morels," *Fungi Magazine,* 2015.
"The Mystery of Disappearing Bees," *Wichita Broadside Proje*ct, 2017, with art by Skyler Lovelace.
"Newly Released, Classified," *Thorny Locust,* 2017.
"Pretense," *River City Poetry* Summer Issue, 2017.
"The prodigal son goes to the disco," *Prompts: A Spontaneous Anthology,* Jeanette Powers and J. D. Tulloch (Editors), 39 West Press, 2016.
"Quail Hunt," *I-70 Review,* 2015.
"Reading *Moby Dick* Again," *Zingara Poetry Review,* 2018
"Refugee Shores," *as* "Rumors of Europe," *365 Days: A Poetry Anthology,* 365 Days Poetry, 2016.
"*Rosarium* Threnody," *Dappled Things,* 2016.
"Ruby (1954)," *Chiron Review,* 2016. Won the 2014 *Jim Stone Memorial Prize for Poetry.*
"Stand by Me," *Pif Magazine,* 2016.
"Staying Warm," *Kansas Voices Anthology,* 2016.
"Sweet, Your Heart," *Mockingheart Review,* 2017.
"tree shadows," *Beecher's Magazine,* 2014, winner, 2014 *Beecher's Poetry Prize* (Frank X. Walker, Judge).
"Under Prairie Skies," *One Sentence Poems,* May 2, 2017.
"Ways of the Wind," *Kansas City Voices,* 2014.
"When Is It Summer in Kansas?" *River City Poetry,* Spring Issue 2018.
"Winter's Weft," *The Lyric,* 2013.

Lastly, thanks to editor, book designer, and publisher Tracy Million Simmons for her enthusiasm and professionalism. It's an honor to have *Stage Whispers* join the Meadowlark Books catalog.

Notes

Stage Whisper— "a loud whisper by an actor that is audible to the spectators but is supposed for dramatic effect not to be heard by one or more of the actors" (*Merriam-Webster Unabridged Dictionary*).

p. 6: In the poem, "Spring, Bittersweet as Separation," *O. Henry* is the pen name of American short story writer William Sydney Porter (1862-1910).

p. 7: "First Holy Communion" contains the phrase "... on the very day when God / came and sat on his tongue..." which alludes to the Roman Catholic Church's doctrine of *Transubstantiation*, which states that once an ordained priest blesses the bread of the Lord's Supper, it is transformed into the actual flesh of Christ (though it retains the appearance, odor, and taste of bread); and when he blesses the wine, it is transformed into the actual blood of Christ (though it retains the appearance, odor, and taste of wine).

p. 8: "Family"—*The Golden Shovel* poetic form was devised by poet Terrance Hayes in homage to poet Gwendolyn Brooks. The last words of each line in a *Golden Shovel* poem are, in order, words from a line or lines taken from another poem, often one by Brooks, in this case, approximating each word of her poem "We Real Cool."

p. 8: *ASARCO* is an acronym for American Smelting and Refining Company, which owned and operated a zinc smelter (Circle Smelting Corp.) from 1904 through 1994 in the author's childhood home town, Beckemeyer, Illinois. The company went through an environmental bankruptcy in 2009; funds were provided to the United States EPA to cover damage at a number of Super Fund sites, including this one, where the operator had "discarded residual metals, coal cinders and slag from the smelting process in piles on the 28-acre property. These disposal practices resulted in elevated concentrations of lead, cadmium, nickel and copper in the soil" (*Circle Smelting Corp. Beckemeyer, IL* Superfund Site web page at https://cumulis.epa.gov/supercpad/cursites/csitinfo.cfm?id=0500350).

p.11: *"En Passant"—* The short story "The Girls in Their Summer Dresses," by Irwin Shaw, appeared in the Feb. 4, 1939, issue of *The New Yorker* (pp. 17-19). I read it in the early 1960's, and it stuck with me all these years.

p. 12: "Anderson Creek Creed" refers explicitly to the doctrine of *Transubstantiation* (see note above for p. 7). It was apparently on my mind for a while. The Anderson Creek wildfire burned nearly 400,000 acres in Kansas and Oklahoma in March 2016.

p. 16: "Grain Elevator Gray" is another *Golden Shovel* poem, this one inspired by Liz Berry's poem, "Birmingham Roller." Her poem is an ode to that British breed of pigeons that can somersault in flight. The last words in each line of my poem match hers.

p. 17: "Above the Rocky Run"—To *ferry* a canoe or kayak is to paddle it upstream at an angle to the current so that the current pushes the boat sideways across the stream.

p. 19: "jack 1941-1959." My brief essay, "Poetry, Memoir, and 'Biomythography,'" at the *Whispering Prairie Press* website (http://www.wppress.org/poetry-memoir-and-biomythography/), discusses the origins of this poem.

p. 25: "For Billie Holiday" refers to two of the songs that Billie Holiday made famous, "Good Morning Heartache," which was written by Irene Higginbotham, Ervin Drake, and Dan Fisher, and originally recorded by Billie in 1946. "Strange fruit hangin' from poplar trees" is a line from the song "Strange Fruit," written by Abel Meeropol and recorded by Billie Holiday in 1939. It became her signature song even though its lyrics, protesting lynchings of blacks, were controversial at that time. The last line, "Use the alley door, if you please," refers to the practice in the 1940's and 1950's, of venues requiring that Negro performers enter only through back entrances.

p. 56: "Four Old Barns"—A *purlin* is a horizontal structural element that supports rafters in a roof.

p. 73: "Morel" Mushrooms of the genus *Morchela*, called morels, are highly prized for their flavor. Patches of them are jealously guarded by connoisseurs. Aradids are insects, true bugs of the family Aradidae, that feed on fungi.

p. 79: "This Poetry"—The *Ovijello* is an old Spanish poem form: 10 lines comprising 3 couplets and a quatrain with rhyming pattern aa/bb/cc/cddc. Each couplet with the first line 8 syllables, second line 3 or 4, first line a question or statement, second line an answer or echo. The final line of the quatrain repeats lines 2, 4, and 6.

p. 91: The last line in "*Rosarium* Threnody" is taken from the Roman Catholic traditional prayer, the "Hail Mary," which goes, in its entirety: "Hail Mary, full of grace, the Lord is with thee; blessed art thou amongst women, and *blessed is the fruit of thy womb*, Jesus. Holy Mary, Mother of God, pray for us sinners, now and at the hour of our death, Amen."

My essay on the origins of this poem, "Coping through Connections: Faith, rationality, and poetry," appeared in *Chrysalis: Journal of Transformative Language Arts*, in 2016: http://www.tlanetwork.net/2016/10/coping-through-connections-faith-rationality-and-poetry-by-roy-j-beckemeyer/.

p. 99: "Plath's Children"—Poet/author Sylvia Plath committed suicide in 1965. Found with her head in the oven, she had kept the gas from reaching her children's room by sealing off the kitchen with wet cloths.

The Author

Roy Beckemeyer and his wife, Pat, live in Wichita, Kansas. His poems have appeared in half a dozen anthologies as well as in a variety of print and on-line journals including *Beecher's Magazine*, *The Bluest Aye*, *Chiron Review*, *Coal City Review*, *Dappled Things*, *Flint Hills Review*, *Fungi*, *I-70 Review*, *Kansas City Voices*, *The Light Ekphrastic*, *The Midwest Quarterly*, *Mikrokosmos*, *Mockingheart Review*, *The North Dakota Quarterly*, *Pif*, *River City Poetry*, *The Syzygy Poetry Review*, *Thorny Locust*, *Tittynope 'Zine*, and *Zingara*. His first book of poetry, *Music I Once Could Dance To* (Coal City Press, Lawrence, KS, 2014) was selected as a Kansas Notable Book. Two poems from that book were Pushcart Prize nominees. He was co-editor with Caryn Mirriam-Goldberg, Kansas Poet Laureate Emerita, of *Kansas Time+Place: An Anthology of Heartland Poetry* (Little Balkans Press, Pittsburg, Kansas, 2017). His chapbook of ekphrastic poems, *Amanuensis Angel*, was recently published by Spartan Press (Kansas City, MO, 2018). He was President of the Kansas Authors Club from 2016-2017 and was KAC Poet of the Year in 2013, and 2015 -2017. He won the Kansas Voices Poetry Award in 2016.

WWW.MEADOWLARK-BOOKS.COM

Specializing in Books by Authors from the Heartland since 2014

GREEN BIKE

MoonStain
poetry by Ronda Miller

LIKE BUDDHA-CALM BIRD

Water Signs
poetry by Ronda Miller

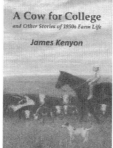
A Cow for College
and Other Stories of 1950s Farm Life
James Kenyon

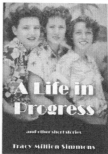
A Life in Progress
and other short stories
Tracy Million Simmons

To Leave a Shadow
Michael D. Graves

Songs for my Father
a collection of poems & stories
by Kevin Rabas

Walking on Water
poems by Cheryl Unruh

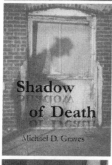
Shadow of Death
Michael D. Graves

What Lies Beyond

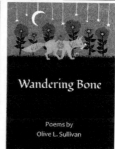
Wandering Bone
Poems by Olive L. Sullivan

Everyday Magic
Field Notes on the Mundane and the Miraculous
Caryn Mirriam-Goldberg

When Creation Falls
Poems by Roy Wasserstein

DRIVING TOGETHER